ESCAPE
- OR -
EVADE

COL. DAVID W. IRVIN, JR.

TURNER PUBLISHING COMPANY

Turner Publishing Company

Copyright © 2002 Col. David W. Irvin, Jr.
Publishing Rights: Turner Publishing Company

Turner Publishing Company Staff:
Ginny Forstot, Publishing Consultant

Library of Congress Control No.: 2002101469

ISBN: 978-1-68162-295-8

Limited Edition.

Contents

The Route

Evreux

Rouen

Amiens

Lille

St. Quental

Ghent

Antwerp

Dordrecht

Eindhoven

Rotterdam

Den Helder

Wadden Zee

Holmwerd

Ribe

Kolding

Nyborg

Korsor

Slagelse

Copenhagen

Odense

Malmo

Prologue

This book begins with the disabling of an American bomber in 1943. When the bomber starts to disintegrate after being crippled by enemy gunfire and plunges towards the earth, the crewman's motions become automatic if the flier is determined to survive a crash. After the individual departs the crippled plane, the training, such as it was at the beginning of WWII, begins to come to the surface to most of those who were involved. Quite frankly, in the early days of WWII there was no way to train the flight crews how (or when) to leave a crippled aircraft. I remember that somewhere in my flight training I was told "if" I had to bailout, it was best to jump from the aircraft with your arms wrapped around your legs in "a ball," as it were. The problem with this is that those of us who had to use the chest pack because of the necessity to move about, had to keep the chute next to them so they could hook it up under normal circumstances.

If the aircraft is stable, getting the chute into the harness is no problem. If the aircraft is gyrating, just getting the chest chute in your hands is a chore and hooking it up to the connecting hooks can really cause a lot of trouble. Let's assume the chute is in place, then the problem is getting out of the aircraft and trying to remember to grasp your legs with your arms. Remember, the chest chute is on your chest. Assuming all this is done, then you have to recognize when to pull the ripcord.

The individual has to be under control to save himself. If he pauses, it is too late. All the events are capsulated in time. It has to be a controlled situation.

If the flier is fortunate to remember his cloth helmet and it is left on (that protects the ears and has the radio gear) the head bounces all over and the pain sharpens the mind. To put it in perspective, consider putting on all your clothes while you are driving on the centerline of the highway at 50 miles per hour, all in the space of 10 seconds or you can expect to lose your life. Now consider what happens if your vehicle is tumbling. Unless you have experienced this, there is no way to envision what is happening, what is going to happen next, how you are going to get out of the accident (or worse), when and most importantly, if.

Now that the decision is made for you to get out of the aircraft, consider you have to hook up your chest parachute, assuming you are wearing a parachute harness. If you are not, the only hope is that your will has been written and is in order. Putting on the chest chute is a simple matter, but consider it is like being thrown about in the back seat of your car and all you have to do is hook (twice) a 25 pound weight onto the harness. Of course, the chute must be placed in the right position, but doing that only takes only three or four tries and remember you have just been bounced against the wall, repeatedly. If the plane is spinning, centrifugal force can hold you against the wall of the crawl way and you have to fight your way in the direction of the bomb bay, the direction you need to go. Time is not something to keep in mind. You have to keep moving because the airplane can come apart (or explode) at any time.

The aches and pains aren't impeding your movement to be able to exit the aircraft through an eight foot long crawl way (from the bombardiers station) three feet high and three feet wide, being thrust from side to side, top to bottom, till you're through and have to worm your way around the base of the top turret gunners position to the bomb bay. If the bomb bay door is open you can claw your way through, still within the 10 seconds allocated and throw yourself out of the opening, afterwards thinking someone who opened the door should be thanked. Now you have to dive out and hope the open doors don't cut off your arms or legs. Then you find yourself shuttling through space. Clearing the open bomb bay doors is not easy. The aircraft is gyrating and I remember hitting my left shoulder on the right bomb bay door, but not to the extent that I was crippled, although it hurt. Once clear of the aircraft, you try to remember to keep your arms crossed over the top of the chute. Also, it is imperative to keep the legs together and toes pointing. While gyrating, you try to look up and hope to see the blue sky. If you are lucky to be in that position, you violently pull the chute ripcord. The reason for this is so that the parachute opens when you are literally flat on your back, with nothing to impede its opening and you won't get slapped by the opening parachute.

Quite frankly, I do not remember leaving the gyrating plane. The first thing I do remember is going from dark (inside the plane), to the sudden light that shocked the whole body, even though you're not aware of what is up or down.

You look at what you think is up, finally see your airplane against the horizon, having lost a wing but still not on fire, in a steeping dive. I distinctly remember not seeing anyone else getting out.

Before the reader considers the movement of the escapee/evadee, it must be remembered the bailout of the crew members, at this time, was long before the ejection seat and is totally different from leaving a fighter plane.

With all this in mind, let the story begin.

Chapter One:

The Capture

NOVEMBER 19, 1943

everal lead crew members were sent to the 8th Air Force preceding a new bomber group's deployment to Great Britain. This was done in secrecy, to (1) protect the fact that US was sending new units to the European Theater of Operations (ETO) and (2) to give the new units experience they would have not otherwise have obtained.

The 447th Bomb Group (Heavy) was flying the B-17G, the latest model of the best bomber in the world. (Yes, I have flown the B-29; it flew higher and faster and carried a bigger bomb load, but I would rather fly the B-17 than the B-29 any time.) We were flying all kinds of missions from Harvard, NE including over-water submarine patrol (from Galveston, TX) over the Gulf of Mexico.

The group was scheduled to go from Harvard to Grand Island, NE for our POE (Point of Embarkation) where we were to fill out paperwork, get new issues of flying suits, high altitude boots, new electrical suits (never long enough), flak suits and helmets. I got my new equipment before the unit left for the POE.

Unfortunately, when the entire unit (three squadrons) performed a group flyby at Harvard, the squadron leader (low squadron) got out of control, crashed and burned in front of a small group of unit and base personnel. The crew was killed. The pilot was a West Point graduate. The investigation called the disaster "pilot error." On the ground, the pilot was unapproachable. Fortunately, I was not in his squadron. He didn't fly regularly and that is essential when flying close formation.

In retrospect, the only phase not of our combat crew training was formation flying. This was understandable, because no one had been used to the combat "box" that was designed by LEMay. We never got close to another B-17, that was a mistake of great proportions. Assembling 21 bombers, separating them into three squadrons, the lead, the high and the low was a feat we didn't have time for. Supposedly, we would get that training in England. Loss of one aircraft with 10 crew members was not something that was condoned; however, it was inevitable considering the lack of expertise on the part of the new crews.

At approximately 2:15 p.m. my crew and I were shot down by a German Me-109 west of Paris, France. The shock was doubly severe because I was flying with a 94th BG arrived for combat duty with the 8th Air Force at RAF Station 126, at Rattlesden, south of Norwich. I was attached to the Group Headquarters (supposedly, I found out, for security reasons, on leave while there) and assigned to fly with different crews. I had no objection to this for it was in this way I could get experience in my position.

Riding in the nose, as a replacement bombardier, I was on my third overseas combat mission. The first two flights were "milk runs," as they were called, because they were short in duration and not over a heavily defended target. The 447th was to become a part of the 4th Combat Wing, along with the 94th BG at Bury, St. Edmunds and the 385th BG located at Great Ashfield.

Our aircraft was flying number three in that high squadron. That meant we were stationed above and to the left of the lead flight.

The high squadron was to the left of the squadron lead. The lead squadron (six aircraft) took off first, followed by the high squadron (us) with six aircraft and then the low squadron with six aircraft. Lastly, the spare aircraft took off, who positioned himself above the main force. Radio silence between aircraft was enforced. If an aircraft was unable to continue, the crew would fire a red flare, drop out of formation and head back to their home base. The spare would then maneuver into the vacant position and the group would continue.

I watched the maneuvering from my position. We had to

circle the field three times to get all of our aircraft into their proper position. At the end of the third circle, the lead co-pilot who flew in the tail position, advised the plane commander (who was flying in the co-pilot's seat) when all of the planes were in position. The left seat was the commander's seat, whether it was the pilot or if the unit was leading the formation, was usually the group director of operations, the vice commander or the commander. Otherwise, it was the crew pilot. The lead plane of the group would then fire a green-green flare. Sounds complicated, but these crews were veterans and knew what and when to do things. All I had to do was to watch.

The weather was clear and cold. After our group formation was in place, we got the green flare to proceed to the rendez-vous with the two other groups that comprised the 4th Combat Wing. We saw them ahead and above us, so we maneuvered the 21 planes to fall in to the left and atop the other two units. Another green flare and the entire combat box headed out over the English Channel. We were flying at 23,000 feet. As we crossed the coast of France, the top turret gunner (I assumed that's who it was, he didn't identify himself) announced, "German fighters at 11 O'clock high." I looked up to the left, but couldn't see anything, then I saw them, coming out of the sun. I heard the top turret gunner firing his .50 caliber guns.

Three Me-109s were headed for the lead group. I fired several bursts with no effect. I remembered that our group was going to have incendiary bullets for every three shells. That should help the gunners to see where their bullets were going. This group fired no incendiaries. The number three B-17 of the lead squadron started to smoke from the No. 1 engine. But he kept in formation. The engine kept smoking and I saw that the pilot had feathered the engine, but stayed in the lead formation.

The ball turret gunner called "three Me-109's, 4 O'clock low coming at us." I looked down and as far back as I could, but couldn't find them. Suddenly, the plane lurched and I could hear bullets hitting our left wing. We slewed to the left and dropped the left wing. The B-17F was on fire between the No. 1 and 2 engines, we rapidly began to lose altitude. We were generally heading west, on our return to England. I bumbled my way back to the bomb bay and found the bomb bay doors open, but no one was there. My chest chute (the only ones who used the backpacks were the two pilots) and our chest chute was close nearby. For some reason, most of the crew had to move about quite often.

For some reason (I don't remember why) I delayed pulling the ripcord immediately after clearing the aircraft. I was tumbling, so I thought it was time to use the chute, pulled the ripcord and felt the chute pack pass my face, slapping me about the face. I looked up and saw silk blossoming and I immediately stopped gyrating. The earth was right-side up and my arms were over my head. My legs were spread far apart. This was not the way we were taught.

I looked down, for the first time and saw the ground, trees and figures running my way pointing at me. I finally remembered my parachute training, bringing my head up, looking straight ahead and focusing on the trees ahead of me. I brought my legs together and flexed my knees.

The ground came up faster than I expected. When I struck the ground I fell to one side, rolling over and holding onto the parachute cords. There was no wind, so my chute collapsed around me. I vaguely remember looking up at the white silk, I was on my back and then heard voices. Next, the chute was ripped from my body and I was staring at the muzzle of a rifle being held by a German solider wearing a steel helmet. He said to get up and raise my hands (I spoke some German).

There were four soldiers in dark green uniforms, black belts and jackboots. One of them searched me from head to toe and finding nothing of value, pointed towards a large group of trucks in the distance. Two of them prodded me in the back with their rifles and we moved towards the others. As we came closer, I noticed we were being shepherded towards a camouflaged flak battery with several trucks and several camouflaged tents. The guns were manned and quite a few shell casing were strewn around the battery of three large caliber guns.

I was hustled into the rear seat of one of the weapon carriers with two of the soldiers with me. The driver took off down a rough dirt road. About 10 minutes later we were waved through a gate and entered what looked like an airfield. There was a control tower with mesh covering the tower supports and a fluttering windsock. While driving slowly, suddenly the truck stopped with me and the guard in back. I looked up and saw a German officer approaching the truck holding his hand up, signifying "stop." He came to the back of the truck, said something to the guard and came right in front of me. He glared and pulled my head back by yanking my hair so I was up against the side wall of the vehicle. I didn't know what to expect. He spat in my face and I reacted by lunging for his neck, arms extended. The guard reacted immediately and shoved the rifle he was carrying in my stomach. I collapsed. The officer kicked me in the ribs, again said something to the guard, jumped down from the truck waving the driver to "drive on" and went towards the control tower, swaggering as he went. As he passed the gun emplacement, the four gunners came to attention and saluted. He casually returned the salute.

I started to shake all over and the guard laughed, but did nothing else. After a short period, I gained control and put my head down between my knees. I was feeling queasy and thought I might throw up, but did not.

All of the one-story buildings were painted and camouflaged. There were soldiers everywhere. They appeared to be quite casual when they saw me in the truck. We pulled up in front of a large building with two guards protecting the entrance. I was shoved out of the back into the building and pushed into an office with an officer seated behind a large desk. I was asked the usual questions in German and then waved off. The guards grabbed me and wrestled me back to the truck, literally throwing me in the back seat and hitting me with the butts of their rifles.

After riding in several directions, we pulled up in front of a small concrete building with a guard in front. The guard opened a large metal door and I was again manhandled inside and was hit several times in the back. I was by now in a lot of pain and was thrown into a small, narrow cell. No lights, no windows and one blanket. That was all. The door was slammed shut and bolted. I could think of nothing but the pain in my back. I thought, I hope my kidneys are okay (they were). It was starting to get dark, yet it was only 4 p.m. My watch was still working and they hadn't take it from me. Why I'll never know. I suddenly felt a cold wave come over me and I lurched forward trying to reach the blanket, but fell to my knees. Vaguely, I remember crawling on hands and knees and threw the blanket around me, sitting up against the wall.

I pulled the blanket around me and tried to get some sleep. Sleep was impossible. I was so tense I couldn't relax, so I tried to concentrate on one subject, to get my mind focused. In my thoughts I kept thinking my captors were waiting for something to happen. I decided they were waiting from someone of higher authority to tell them what to do with me. The thought passed my mind this was 1943 and quite a lot of Germans were not indoctrinated in handling POWs. I didn't know they had set up a POW processing center in Frankfurt, Germany and from there were assigned to camps throughout Germany, Prussia, Czechoslovakia, Austria and the like.

In the distance I could hear the sound of aircraft engines coming and going. Soon it was dark (from the lights being "on" in the corridor), so they must have been night fighters based at this airfield. Transport planes had a deep rumbling sound. Fighters, on the other hand, had a high pitched noise. This was my observation of our aircraft and thought the Germans had the same. Late in the evening I heard the sound of machine guns in the distance, this continued for about an hour and then there was silence. The sound of aircraft told me the Germans were indeed operating night fighters out of the base.

Later that night, two more aircraft took off but I did not hear them land. The planes, whatever they were, kept my mind away from the fact that I was in enemy hands and probably would be taken to an interrogation center and then to a POW camp. Something to look forward to. Finally, I fell asleep only to be awakened by a short, gruff-sounding guard who motioned me outside. It was getting light. He followed me to a barbed wire enclosure about 100 yards by 75 yards. There were guards walking around the outside of the enclosure. Apparently, this was an exercise yard. I walked the perimeter, using the time to measure the length and width and to get the stiffness out of my legs. The pain in my back had subsided, but was still tender to the touch. There was no one in the enclosure but me.

As I was walking near the concrete blockhouse, there were the sounds of many engines off in the distance. I turned around and saw six B-26 medium bombers very low and fast. They were coming in from the west. I had heard enough B-26 engines to recognize them. Each aircraft had its sound. The leading plane was coming directly at us. The German gunners were firing fast and furiously. Suddenly one B-26 was hit and dropped a wing. It looked as if it was going to hit me. He dropped his bombs and pulled up out of formation. I dropped flat against the concrete building. When the bombs hit, the concussion threw me hard against the concrete wall. The aircraft wallowed out of sight still flying on one engine, smoke coming from the other.

Still dazed I got to my feet and saw the guards had vanished. One of the bombs obliterated part of the barbed wire enclosure and without thinking, I ran to the open ground and headed away from the base and runway, sighting a grove ahead of me in the distance. No soldiers around, but the flak batteries behind me were still shooting at the departing medium bombers. I kept running, no one was around; I stumbled several times and finally lay prone on the ground. From my position I could see soldiers trying to put out the fires caused by exploding bombs. There was an open space between the base and me, but I couldn't move. It must have been a delayed reaction to the bomb blast that made way for me to escape. My mind was functioning but my limbs were "on hold." I lay there trying to move to the protection of the underbrush. However, my legs would not cooperate. Panic was starting to set in.

In what seemed like an eternity, my fingers started to move, then my arms. Finally my feet regained their feel, then my legs, then my hips. The panic I was feeling must have helped. There I was out in the open, in sight of the Germans. Fortunately, the B-26s had done their job (I wondered about the one who had been hit in one engine, hoping he made it back safety) and their bombing had diverted their attention away from me.

I felt naked, but raised my knees and crawling, falling down several times.

Chapter Two

The Escape

OCTOBER 19-20, 1943

*T*he trees were thick. I picked myself up and plunged into the grove. There were bushes all over and a growth of vines. I laid on my back, staring through the tree branches at the blue sky. It was now 11 a.m. and things had quieted down considerably. The only thing was the smell of smoke. I started to cough, then stifled it with my hand and rolled onto my side.

The sun was overhead and it was getting warm. I unzipped my leather flying jacket, it was still warm, but more comfortable. Amazing as it may sound, I still had my flying jacket, flying suit, boots and watch! I found out much later, that it was not uncommon to remove the prisoners boots as a deterrent to trying to escape. Apparently, this base was not ready to handle captured allied fliers who were captured and put under guard.

During many of our many briefings, not a word was said about what the Germans did with our clothing. The Americans were figuratively youngsters in the POW business. For example, on my own I sewed a compass, a silk map and some matches in my flying suit. The map I got from the Intelligence folks showed western, northern and southern Europe. The issued Escape and Evasion Kit in a plastic sealed pouch was the first thing the Germans confiscated. I never understood why they didn't take my watch and boots, they made a big mistake, but I didn't realize it until later.

I must have dozed off. I saw the sun was getting low in the west. It was quiet, no aircraft sounds and no sounds of people or vehicles. I wondered if they had forgotten me. Not likely. I couldn't see any soldiers on this side of the base. I suddenly realized I was an escapee in extremely unfriendly territory. Worst of all, I was on my own.

We had not been briefed on what to do solo, or how we were to get in contact with the Resistance, especially when I was in my flying gear. Rather obvious. We were briefed on how to get to Spain or Switzerland, but doing so seemed so unlikely. I dismissed it from my mind. We were not told to go to Sweden. Rather, we were specifically briefed NOT to go to Sweden, for they were rigidly neutral and wanted nothing that could make the Nazis upset. Interestingly enough, nothing was said about Denmark or Norway.

After my initial ordeal, I thought about the E&E Kit and I got mad, because if we were captured, we would lose our capability to escape or evade. We would really be on our own! An absorbing thought.

My mind was clearing and I started to piece together the parts of the flight that told me where I was. Leaving the English Channel eastbound, our target was LeBourget airfield in Paris, but we never got there. Swarms of Me-109s, Fw-190s and even a few Me-110s jumped us before we got to the run in point. The pilot I was flying with turned west and started to lose altitude, followed by a half dozen fighters (we had no escorts; the Spitfires had to turn back because of low fuel) who were bound and determined we would not get away.

By my mental calculations (and sparse training) the airfield was Evreux-Fauville, the town of Evreux was northwest. Rouen was a fairly large city and was in the north. It had a railroad, my primary objective at this point. Our escape and evasion route was to Spain over the Pyranees Mountains. According to the intelligence people, the Resistance was strong and could get us away when (and if) we could get in contact with them. The railway at Rouen headed northeast and southwest. Rouen was it, for my purposes. I had to get to the train heading southwest. But first, I had to get there and find some way to get a ticket. I had a limited amount of Belgian and French money sewed into my flying suit. The Germans missed the paper money during their search. They immediately took my plastic Escape and Evasion Kit, which wasn't surprising. Rouen was about 30 miles. I figured if I could get there before the sun came up, I would be okay, but I had to do at least five miles per hour and that wasn't logical.

Heading north (stars are wonderful guideposts, if you know what you're doing), I started out across country. Soon I saw a path with a farm ahead. Approaching slowly, I remember farms had dogs, but I heard nothing. In the barn, I found a bicycle, that was my way out, I thought. I pedaled furiously trying to distance myself, keeping to the road.

My thoughts raced ahead, but I was frustrated by the fact I couldn't get any civilian clothes from the farmhouse barn. My flight suit, leather jacket and high-top boots were a dead give-away, but I had to get to that train and distance myself from any pursuing soldiers. Maybe I could find a civilian who was not in alliance with the Germans. Better yet, possibly I could come across a Resistance fighter.

Chapter Three
The Contact

OCTOBER 21, 1943

*a*bout 20 minutes had passed and my legs were aching from the pedaling. I could see lights ahead and I stopped, looking for something recognizable. I saw a railroad track embankment and hurried towards it.

Reaching the tracks, I turned right (towards the north) towards the town. Following the tracks I saw the railroad station dimly lit. I dropped the bicycle in a grove of bushes. As I approached the station platform, I saw a group of young men (students, I guess) with a tall elderly man (obviously the leader) in their midst. I approached him. He was much taller than most of the students and considerably older. He was facing me and saw me immediately. He motioned me toward the group of young men. At this time I heard the train coming from the west. Because of height I was head and shoulders above the boys, so I bent down to keep me from being conspicuous. It is interesting to note most Europeans are short in height. I am six foot, three inches and that made a big difference. Most of those I saw or met where about five feet, eight inches. The boys, who looked like college students (they were) kept whispering amongst themselves and that made me very nervous. I wanted to yell to keep quiet, but the train was coming into the station and the noise calmed me down. Unfortunately, I thought, the train was heading north and I wanted to go south as briefed. I had no time to worry about that. I was considerably fortunate to find someone who would help me, dressed in flying clothes as I was.

The elderly leader, gray hair, mustache, goatee and wearing a brown suit, came directly to me and said in good English, "We come from Nantes, going to Ghent. You are welcome to join us." That was it for now. He turned away, whispering to the students.

With the help of the boys, I boarded the train and found plenty of seats. The elderly man sat down opposite me and said, "You will never make it in that outfit." I then realized I was in my flight gear and jacket. "I am Dr. Bergeron, returning to the University of Ghent. Talk to no one," and handed me a pair of trousers, shirt, coat and cap, plus my ticket. "Pretend to be asleep when the conductor comes by. Put your ticket in your cap. Change clothes now and give me your flight gear."

Changing swiftly, handing my old gear to the student, I immediately felt tired, but remembered I had sewn a compass in my sleeve and had the paper money to retrieve. I told the professor and he said something to the student who had my gear. He nodded and moved towards the water closet and disappeared. He returned giving me the compass, but not the money. The doctor patted me on the knee and I feel asleep shortly thereafter. At 9:15 the train stopped at Amiens and we changed trains. I was surrounded by the students as we changed. One of the older students, who spoke broken English, told me we had to change because the train tracks had been blown up between Amiens and Lille. We were rerouted through St. Quental. There weren't any inspections on the new train. I took a nap before our last stop and that perked me up. I started remembering. I was extremely lucky because of the bombers and because I had been slow in getting to the initial train station. Otherwise, I would have missed the professor and his students. My luck was holding, I hoped.

We went through Lille without stopping and arrived at Roubaix at 10:30 p.m. For the first time we were inspected by the Belgian police in non-descript uniforms and caps. They did not ask for our papers or identification and the train got underway immediately. I was scared by the police, but they appeared to be unconcerned.

I leaned against the side of the compartment and was soon asleep again. We rocked back and forth. I heard the others chattering and the doctor had his eyes shut, but still sitting close to me.

I was awakened by the slowing of the train. Dr. Bergeron leaned towards me and said, "We are arriving at Ghent. Get prepared for a fast exit." The time was 3:30 a.m. The train slowed down and before we reached the center of the station, the students started jumping off. The doctor was behind me and he literally pushed me through the doorway. I hit the ground running. The professor had never left my shoulder. Students were running in all directions, some going past us in a rush.

The overhead lights were very dim, but the students seemed to know to get out of the station. Somewhere along the melee, the doctor and I separated, but I saw him ahead gesturing to the students to keep moving.

The main entrance to the Bahnhof, or railway station in German, was in the center of the town. As we left the station, no one appeared to be there. Then I remembered it was about 4 a.m.

We slowed down and walked about two miles through the downtown shops with no lights visible and still no one in sight except for a lone patrolman batting the side of the sidewalk with his nightstick periodically. He didn't seem aware there were 14 young men walking past him in the center of the empty street. After what seemed an eternity, we came to a large stone wall and passed through a small recessed door. We were at the university.

The older student (the one who loaned me his clothes, was one of the taller of the students) touched my shoulder and motioned for me to follow him. We went down a darkened stairway. I was still bent over, so I straightened up and the pain in my back almost caused me to fall over. The student steadied me and led me to a room under the stairs, very small, but had a cot with pillow, no toilet and no window. He told me his name was Eric. He said I should rest and food would be brought to me in two hours. With that, he left and closed the door, softly. It was suddenly quiet with a small light bulb providing what light there was. I couldn't find any light switch, so I laid down and faced the wall. The next thing I remembered was a young girl gently shaking me. She said nothing, but pointed to a tray of food on the washstand. With that, she smiled, turned about and left. There were two pieces of rye bread (no butter), a small piece of smelly cheese, two raw carrots and coffee. The food was delicious and like one who hadn't eaten for two days, I cleaned the plates and even enjoyed the strange tasting coffee. I found out later it was made from dried ground acorns, prevalent in Europe. It was bitter but sweetened by dried and crushed beets.

There was a knock on the door, I must have fallen asleep again. I opened the door and the young girl brushed by me, picked up the dishes and tray and left, closing the door behind her. The time was 5:15 p.m. I sat down on the bed with my back against the wall. The position relieved my back, somewhat. I reviewed what had happened and realized I was headed north when I wanted to go south to Spain. No one came that night and I slept soundly.

Being left alone, my thoughts naturally went to where I was going, where I was and how long was I staying. These thoughts flooded my brain. I must get the answers to these questions before I could find the calmness that was not in my nature. At the time, instinct was my only companion. I do remember, vividly, the viciousness of the Nazi officer, but there was no fear. I was alone, as I had been for much of my life. My parents were divorced when I was 9 and I lived with my mother in San Francisco. She worked to support us and was only home at night. My father and I did not have contact until much later.

Chapter Four
The Plan
OCTOBER 26-27, 1943

Nothing occurred for the next two days, except I was shown where the toilet was. I took a sponge bath, slept, ate and wondered what the hell was going on.

An elderly woman knocked on my door around 3 p.m. with a bundle of clothes, very non-descript and included a well-prepared of thick stockings. She laid the clothes on the bed, smiled, touched my arm and left shutting the door. I never learned her name, but Eric told me she lost her 25 year-old son to the Germans and she would help me to escape.

Eric and the professor came to my room in the afternoon and helped me to understand what was going to happen. I was to go from Ghent to Antwerp and Rotterdam. The professor handed me travel orders, identification and railroad tickets. There was no picture with the ID card, but that would be taken care of later on. I expressed my concern that I was not going to Spain. Eric smiled and explained the Resistance chain (to the south) had been compromised and it took several weeks to set up the northern route. Although it was more dangerous, I would be taken to Sweden. I told the professor I wasn't happy with the idea of being interned by the Swedes, he held up his hand and told me they were working on it and wouldn't let me be caught. I wasn't satisfied with that explanation, but the professor interrupted me by saying that I was in good hands and not to worry.

I was not given a razor or my hair cut on purpose. My scruffy appearance was an asset. I was to be an engineer, going to Denmark to work in the shipyards for the Kriegsmarine (German navy). My name, in my papers, was William Harth. We were to leave tomorrow night, October 27. Eric, in a whisper, told me "they" had been in touch with London and were told I was to be considered a priority for return as soon as possible.

Eric took me by the arm, went up the stairs into a room halfway down a long hallway. No one else was there. Eric knocked on the door. A young man appeared and motioned me to come in. I immediately noticed two lights and a stool with a camera on a tripod. The young man sat me down on the stool, straightened my tie and pointed to the camera. He took my picture using a flashbulb. Eric escorted me back to my room and left me there, alone again. It was very quiet and a good time to think about what was going on. I was amazed at the efficiency of the Belgians who had befriended me at the risk of their lives. It is easy to just take things as they come, but their unspoken sacrifices were preying on my mind. The camera (who knows how they got that), the film (even more difficult to obtain) and the flashbulbs (an unbelievable asset) all were used to help others. What was amazing to me was the fact that people were organizing a chain of helpers to get we fighters (they were fighting in their own way) to return to our units. I still cannot believe their effectiveness and will always remember each one of them.

Eric, three students and I left at 5:00 p.m. I never got a chance to thank the professor. Walking to the station was the reverse of the way we got to the university. Eric bought four tickets and we showed our identification cards to the local policeman and he barely looked at my card or me, waving me through the vestibule.

There were others on the platform. Most of them were older. The train pulled in at 6:15 p.m. and left a few minutes later. The four of us got aboard in a third class compartment. We were by ourselves. The conductor took our tickets without any fanfare. As we slowly left the station, it was getting dark fast and starting to rain. All the lights in the passenger cars were doused and the conductors used lanterns when they had to. I could see the skyline dimly, as it must have been beautiful in the spring time. There were occasional lights from farmyards, but nothing of any significance. Eric and the three students were napping, so I closed my eyes and got lulled into a sense of security with the rocking of the train and the quiet. I almost forgot what was going on, but my calmness was not becoming habitual, thank goodness.

We arrived at the South Antwerp station at 9:30 p.m. Eric told me we had to change to another train to Eindhoven. We got off the train and stood around. The Eindhoven train arrived at midnight and it was raining hard. We crowded together under the roof and ran to board the train as it stopped. Again, we four were in a third class compartment. There were local police roaming all over the station. I still wonder what they were looking for. Obviously not me.

These people were fighting for three years and it was not easy for us newcomers to understand there are different ways to oppose those who dominated the individual, or the nation for that matter. The lethargy of the Belgians, Dutch and Danes were indicative of their disdain for the Nazi regime.

Occasionally, the German soldiers rode the trains, but this was a gesture in 1943. Fortunately, the Germans couldn't divert many of their people to patrol the "foreign" trains. Lucky for me.

The train was in the depot with all of the lights out, just sitting there at 12:45 a.m. The station lights were out and all we could hear was the hissing of the engine steam. Then in the distance, I heard the sound of aircraft engines, but fortunately they were going somewhere else. It was still raining. The train started up with a lurch at 1:45 a.m. Rotterdam next stop, hopefully.

Shortly thereafter, the train was moving slowly forward, then it slowed more and finally come to a stop. There was no station, no town. Eric leaned over to me and whispered, "Belgian border. Act like you're asleep till they nudge you. If they ask, show them your papers, but don't offer. Slouch down and act sleepy."

The next few minutes were a nightmare. The police checked all of our papers and moved on. As they left to the next car, Eric patted my knee and motioned me to follow him. I had no idea where we were, but I followed him and the three others off the train. We started walking up a dirt road. We kept going in a misty rain until almost 3 a.m. Several trucks went by heading south. We came to a guard station, our clothes sodden. I assumed it was the border between Belgium and Holland. We observed the border from a clump of thick bushes, trying to hide and get out of the rain.

Eric told us to stay where we were. It was raining harder and we crouched together to try to keep warm. We were all soaked through to the skin. Time went by very slowly. I was shaking from the rain, as were the three students. Eric came back three hours later, he was soaked, but had a smile on his face. He led us parallel to the road till we came to a barbed wire fence and we stopped. When a truck came to the checkpoint and while the guards were checking it, we slid below the bottom strand of the barbed wire and fell into a large clump of bushes. About an hour later we got up and still wet to the bone, headed north, I guessed. Eric said he was going to scout ahead. We could see him going towards a small farm with no lights showing. A dog barked and we flattened ourselves in a trench bordering the dirt road.

At 3 a.m., Eric came back with an elderly man who welcomed each of us with a handshake and motioned us to the house. Eric nodded and the four of us trudged across the dirt road. As we entered the house, an elderly lady was standing by a dinner table. She motioned us to sit down, but I headed for the stove to try to dry out. I finally came to the table with relish. Neither of the elderly folks spoke any English, but the food spoke for itself. Boiled potatoes, hot sliced bread, pile of turnips, acorn coffee and a reddish wine. The man said a prayer and we all bowed our heads (I am not religious). The lady started pushing the food around. Eric said we were near a small town of Disodrent, Holland, about 20 kilometers from the outskirts of Rotterdam. I was still wet and by this time the clothes were steaming and had started to dry.

At first I didn't realize the peasant folks had been hoarding their food. They had recently been recruited by the Dutch Resistance and in fact (I found out much later) had received their first, of many, night parachute drops with food and medicine. We were the first to be taken in by them and were just as amateurish as we were. More were established later as part of the "northern" chain of underground workers.

They told us (with Eric as an interpreter) the Germans periodically came to the farm, took eggs, chickens, occasionally a cow and wheat (when in season). He said they were very bitter, having lost their livestock, but more importantly the Germans took their 15 year-old daughter away and they never saw her again (two years). We never did learn their names. They only thing we knew was the couple were survivors of the 1940 Rotterdam disaster, whatever that meant. Apparently, it was very important to Eric. I found out later from Eric, the Resistance gave the parachute units a very hard time when Rotterdam was under siege. The gallant Netherland fighters repulsed the Nazis. After two days the Luftwaffe bombed the city for two days, leveling the city and killed more than 250,000 civilians. The reciprocity was unrelenting.

The food was good and nutritious. The bread was homemade. With the homemade butter lavished on it, I made a pig out of myself. No one argued. The wine was not like anything I had tasted before. The coffee was bitter but warming. As we finished, I realized the food was their only fare, but they were able to exist. It must have been very difficult for them to give to complete strangers. I mentioned this to Eric and he told the couple what I had said. The woman was obviously moved, for she started to cry. She then told Eric she appreciated my concern, but she hated the Nazis. Then she said she and her husband had lived east of Rotterdam and subsisted on what they could raise and hide from the Nazis. They gave sheep to their son when they could. The "Boche" sometimes took several of their sheep, but the son was able to keep a portion of the herd separate and that was how they fed their children and themselves.

It was hot in the small house and I was sleepy. My clothes were slowly drying. Eric led us to the small barn where there was a lot of hay stacked up, plus two cows, but no horses. We nestled down in the loose hay and soon I was asleep in my dirty and damp clothes. We hadn't gotten out of them for three days.

The lady woke us after three hours sleep. I had trouble "getting it together," but stumbled to the back of the barn and relieved myself, much to my embarrassment, for the lady stood there watching me with a smile on her face. I went to the barn door and followed her to the farmhouse. Eric was already seated at the table drinking coffee. We sat down. There were potatoes, cabbage, fresh bread and unbelievably, a chocolate cake with whipped cream! I wondered why and then realized it was her way of saying good-bye, especially for Eric. He was going back and we were going forward, hopefully and back to England.

Chapter Five
The Farm
OCTOBER 30, 1943

I was back in the barn and fell asleep almost immediately. It was 7:30 a.m. before I was wakened by the woman, saying it was time for breakfast. Eric was nowhere to be seen.

At the house the wife said, "Eric ... gone," and sat down to eat. I realized they had waited for us far beyond their normal meal time. We had warm bread, eggs cooked sunnyside up and chicken. All of a sudden the front door opened and there were two men, neither of whom I had seen before. The tall one spoke in French and the short one with a bandage on his cheek, said nothing looking down at the floor. I was still sitting, but I didn't know what else to do.

The tall one looked directly at me and said in English, "I am Robert and this is Harold, a French pilot who was shot down. You and Rene' are going to Denmark." With that, the two of them left. Strange. They went to the barn that was to be our home until we left. The more I thought of the strange way they acted, the more I wondered. But then I realized the whole thing was as new to them as it was to me. The "guides" were feeling their way. This was Robert's first trip, as it turned out. I found out Harold was shot down on his first fighter mission. He had recently completed flight school and had just been assigned to a RAF Hurricane fighter squadron. Not lucky like me.

The weather had taken a turn for the better, so the old man went to the field to harvest alfalfa. The woman was picking the cabbages and digging up potatoes. I wanted to help, but continued to stay out of the open.

I looked through a slit in the barn wall, watching the woman picking the cabbages and putting them in a large basket. The potatoes were lying around in the fading sunlight. After while the French pilot came and patted me on the back. The tall man was not in sight.

The farmer came in and stacked the alfalfa by itself. The lady came in carrying the cabbage, putting it in a bin in the back of the barn. She then went to the storm cellar behind the house. She was not in sight, but smoke was coming from the chimney.

Dinner was being prepared. My thoughts went back to an earlier time. My mother, father, grandfather, grandmother, uncle and two aunts spent three weeks on "the coast," north of Point Reyes, CA on Bolinas Bay in the little hamlet of Gualala. We had a small cabin on the water and Uncle Mike (who ended up as a superior court judge) proclaimed its name to be "Lastima," lazy in Italian. I spent my days playing on the beach or in the hills picking wild strawberries. I learned to watch the cabin chimney. If there was smoke I remember running towards the cabin, for it was near to mealtime. I remember as I was nearing the cabin, the smell of food would cause me to slow down just to smell it longer. Grandma was by far the best cook on a wood stove in the world. The smell from the farm indicated it was time to eat.

Suddenly, the smoke caused to me realize how hungry I was. As Harold and I entered the kitchen I looked for the tall man, but he was not there. The farmer, as though he was reading my thoughts, made a statement in French. Harold said something back in French, then turned to me and said Robert had gone ahead to check our route. Something didn't sound right, but I kept quiet and ate my dinner in silence.

Late that night, about 9 p.m., there was a commotion outside. A dilapidated truck had pulled up. It was between the barn and the house. I laid down but couldn't sleep. I thought at first the Germans had come, but then I saw a woman with gray hair, braided, get out of the cab of the truck and embrace the lady of the farm. They talked in French for several minutes, gesturing towards me. Robert interpreted, "The woman's name is Hette and she will take us to Copenhagen. She has been this way from Den Helder many times and we will leave in three days." I never heard of Den Helder and didn't understand how a Hollander spoke perfect French, but I had no choice. She was in charge. Being 20 years-old, I naturally respected a 50 year-old woman, she was older than my mother.

Chapter Six
The Coffin
NOVEMBER 4, 1943

The next three days dragged. We ate, talked, slept and I wondered if we were ever going to get out of there. I know we must have greatly depleted the food supplies, but they never said anything to us.

The day of the fourth, the farmer, his wife and Hette loaded the old flatboard truck with alfalfa and cabbages. They worked very diligently and we helped. I couldn't help but look at the wood/coal burning engine (boiled water to operate the engine of the truck). The chimney belched black smoke, but wasn't doing anything now, except building up pressure. Hette told Robert we would leave early the next morning. We went back to the barn and tried to relax and get some sleep. I had no idea how long it would be before I would rest again. I doubted I slept more than two hours, but finally 5 a.m. came and we prepared ourselves to get to Rotterdam, only 75 miles, but we were going to be exposed to many Germans. Hette assured us our papers were "good," plus that there were no inspections. We had passed that hurdle already.

In the background I heard the car engine being started and it commenced to "chug." A strange sound, but very unique. Breakfast was a feast! I thought it was the meal before the "big" event. Eggs, hot bread, milk and the usual bitter coffee. It was delicious. Finally, after several cups of coffee, Hette spoke telling us we had to leave.

We approached the truck, its tail engine clamoring and were told to get into the small box with the lid exposed, nestled amid the pile of cabbages. Hette told us we would be 3-1/2 hours on the road, pulling up for inspections before we got to Rotterdam. We would be in a convoy of trucks. We were cautioned to be very quiet when we stopped.

We got in the box. There was little or no room to move. This was going to be tough, I thought. I was tall and had trouble stretching out. Fortunately, Harold was barely five feet tall and the "coffin" was five feet wide, about 5-1/2 feet long and three feet high. We both decided to lay on our backs. My head was opposite Harold's feet. I had to bend my knees. That position didn't give us much motion, but at least we could absorb the bumps. Fortunately, there were several small air holes in each side of the compartment. The smell of the cabbages didn't seem to bother us too much.

The convoy started moving at a slow pace. I immediately smelled the smoke. We pulled out onto the main road and heard several car horns. It had started to turn cold and the rain was getting heavier. The smell permeated the box. We finally slowed down and stopped. We started up again and we had been moving about two hours and the air inside our enclosure was getting heavier. A knock came on the lid, it opened up and the rush of fresh, cold air rushed in. It was intoxicating, but it had started to snow and the wind perked me up. Robert said we better get out and stretch our legs while we could. A sign by the side of the road said Utrecht 13km, that meant we had only gone about 30 miles. The snow was getting heavier.

There were no cars or trucks on the road. The snow obliterated the view and it was getting colder by the minute. Robert said we should get back in the "coffin." Amsterdam was 47 miles beyond. As we climbed aboard, I heard a train close by but couldn't see it.

Once inside I heard the cabbages being piled on top of our hideout. The truck started and we were on our way again. The smoke was still there but the road had begun to smooth out. Eric came by and whispered to be quiet. I could hear the Germans talking to Hette. There was movement, then I could hear bayonets being pushed into the alfalfa on the front part of the truck. Then I felt the truck door slam and there was silence. The Germans had moved off.

Finally, we started to move again. Almost immediately we

crossed a wooden bridge and then turned hard right onto a rocky dirt road. After a short distance, we stopped and Hette yelled at us to be prepared to get out and not to say anything. The cabbages were removed from our "coffin," and we pushed open the lid. We were in a grove of trees. It was dark and snowing. Fortunately, the wind had died down. We were told to get under the truck bed and one of the men threw blankets at us. Hette suddenly appeared from the trees and told Robert we were safe and about a mile south of Amsterdam. No fires, but the trees were thick and gave us some refuge from the snow.

Robert told me that he thought we would go by train the next day. Hette brought us new papers saying she would bring me new ones in the morning. Robert said our present identification would do us no good in Holland or Denmark. We huddled together in the thin blankets for whatever warmth they could provide. My back was acting up and that didn't help getting to sleep.

Escape Or Evade

Chapter Seven
Hette

NOVEMBER 5, 1943

ne of the men roughly pulled us from under the truck and pointed to the first truck. Hette was not in sight. I looked at my watch and found it had stopped because of the wet surroundings for a sustained period. The watch face was clouded with humidity. It was light, but overcast. No snow, no wind, just a quiet solemn picture of three trucks and several men sitting in the cabs of the trucks. It was as if they were all waiting for something. Time went by and it started to snow again.

Out of the gloom a figure emerged bundled up with a hood. The figure looked up. It was Hette. She motioned to the occupants of the three trucks. They all huddled together. Robert interpreted to me what she said in French. Hette said we were going into the outskirts of Amsterdam and spend the day and night in an abandoned factory. We all got into our positions and the trucks backed out of the grove of trees and trundled in tandem to the southern edge of the city. We turned off the main highway and weaved our way through the rubble, obviously a bombed-out factory. The three trucks entered a concrete building with hanging steel girders partially covering an entrance. Once inside, the truck pulled up side by side and the noise of people was evident.

Getting Robert and me aside, Hette told us we were going to separate. She looked directly at me and said (Robert interpreting) she would take Robert and I would go with another Resistance member. I was leaning on the truck bed and my knees almost gave way. I realized I was dependent upon her more than I realized. Robert looked at me and patted my shoulder. She then said I was to leave for Utrecht the next day by walking or riding a bicycle, if it could be found. We were to leave at

6 p.m. We ate cheese, bread and wine, then laid down and tried to sleep. It was a long time coming. I got up and walked around the inside of the concrete walls. This part of Holland had really taken a pounding. The building was once a medium-size factory and my guess was the workers produced something important. It had concrete ceilings, reinforced and the walls were at least two feet thick. The floors were hard, except for the rubble. The machinery had been removed. There were no guards, so the Germans must have decided there was nothing to be salvaged and the building was useless. Not knowing anything about the sub-culture of the Dutch, I didn't know if the absence of graffiti was a true reflection of the people, or they were just too busy. I was to find out later there was a strict curfew throughout Holland, as a from of retribution for the resistance of the Dutch in 1940.

I felt secure in my surroundings. After having gotten through the rigors of the trains and "coffin," this concrete edifice was relaxing and I began to feel I was going to get out of the Nazi-dominated countries. Having cleared France and Belgium, I felt we were definitely making progress. The people of the "northern" route were doing an outstanding job of dodging the Germans so far.

At first those "rebels" were used to dealing with their captors and obviously had learned how to abuse what little freedom they had.

The next morning, Hette, much to my surprise awakened us and motioned Robert and me to follow her. I thought she would be gone by now. We walked (no bicycles) the 10 miles to the town of Utrecht and the railway station was on the south side of town.

Before we started out, Hette gave us our new papers all in order and properly dated. I put my papers in my inner pocket, after being sure I understood who I was. I was still an engineer and came from the town of Avignon, which as I remember, was in the central highlands of France, great grape country. I wasn't sure I could remember who I was, but that would come later.

Hette led the way out of the factory rubble and followed a path to the railroad track and headed generally north. The station that was empty and we passed through the turnstile without any trouble. Two German soldiers were walking by seemingly unconcerned. Hette took hold of my arm, guiding me to a bench against the wall. I took out a piece of cheese and swallowed it. Hette smiled and squeezed my knee. She told us the closer we got to the jump-off point (at this time it was not identified, except for "jump-off point") the more dangerous it would get and the more cautious we had to be. She was visibly nervous, got up and walked to the tracks looking for the train, but nothing was coming. She returned to the bench and told me the train was late but not worry. She was rambling.

The men, dressed in suits, came onto the platform and stood by the tracks. Thirty minutes later, the train crept into the station visibly having been hit by strafing planes, as witnessed by the multiple holes. The train sat still for almost two hours while a train crew repaired the engine and patched the holes they could reach, others they ignored. The compartments were hit pretty hard, but no major damage. We finally were motioned onto the train by the conductor while the train whistle blew several times. Our train was a passenger train with four cars and an engine. I couldn't understand why it was strafed. My mind went back to England. The Spitfires, Hurricanes, the American A-20s, P-38s and P-47s could have spent their time more profitably going after troop and cargo trains, but then I was on the ground and wasn't aware what was going on operationally back home. I was getting too critical, but had to concentrate on getting back and not let my mind wander.

Once seated in the third class compartment with the bullet holes visible, the conductor took our tickets (I don't remember where we were to go or where the train came from). The conductor didn't seem interested in who we were.

The trip was uneventful. We stopped three times and I couldn't tell where we were because it was raining hard and the windows fogged over, plus we had not stopped for more than two minutes at each station. We finally pulled into Den Helder, according to Robert. As we were getting off, I saw more than 30 soldiers in full field gear filing through the exit gate and we filed in behind them. Their smell was overpowering. The guard at the exit point gave my papers a thorough going over and then motioned me through. I don't think they even looked at my face. Robert and Hette were next and the guards rushed us through muttering the smell was terrible.

We followed Hette up one of the small narrow streets until she stopped in front of a non-descript building. She knocked on the door (there were no numbers on any of the buildings). After a few seconds, the door opened and there was a huge blonde man who pulled me into the house, followed by the others in haste and closed the door.

The smoke in the hallway was permeating the whole area. We went down the long hallway and through a door. There was a room full of men, women and a child. The blonde giant motioned us to sit down and immediately everyone started to talk, except the little girl, who came to me, held my hand and smiled.

The blonde man said he was the leader of the Resistance in this area and was working on our escape. He reminded us they were feeling their way, being a "new" escape route. It would take three to five days, depending on the weather. He explained we were going through the Wadden Zee (whatever that meant), by a group of Dutch fishing boats. They had been traveling this route to the northern tip of Holland to Holdwen, a fishing village across the English Channel to net fishing grounds near southwestern Denmark. That statement perked me up. If my geography seemed to be sketchy, it is true that the location of our check points were not given to me ahead of time. Until we reached Amsterdam, I was purposely kept in the dark for one good (and obvious) reason. I was not to be trusted until I "proved" myself. Apparently, I made no covert moves, so I finally was accepted for what I was and not an infiltrator. As a result of the "southern" route compromise, these Resistance people were on edge and didn't trust anyone they didn't know. My arrival was pure coincidence, but they were taking no chances. I was under scrutiny every stop of the way. Besides all the security, I was not allowed to have (or see) a map. I was kept completely in the dark. The guides would tell me what they wanted me to know. As a matter of fact, the western part of Holland and Denmark were not within the area of what little expertise I had.

The sacrifices of these ultimate patriots was not reported with any degree of depth until years after the end of the European part of WWII. Their effort saved thousands of lives and I for one, recognize their devotion to duty and have dedicated this book to them even at this late date.

The men in the room were fishing boat captains, the women were their wives. This, then, was the Resistance group in charge. According to what I understood from the intelligence briefing back in England, resistance groups acted individually and when needed, worked within their "cell," or group to do what was necessary. This was much different, more dangerous because obviously the cell was together and could be compromised. But at this point, I wasn't going to say anything. However, I was going to have to be more careful than I had been before.

The blonde man said he was the leader of the Resistance in this area and was working on our escape. He emphasized this again and again, sometimes pounding the table. He went on to explain they had to traverse the German estuary coming from Wilhelmshaven to the North Sea. It was vigorously protected, continuously by fast E-boats. Thus far, he said, the Germans had sunk four British submarines who were trying to get into the shipyards further inland.

The blonde man (we were never told his name by his request), brought out a weathered map and traced the route we would be taking. He said timing and the weather were the keys, hence the three to five day delay. Apparently, the channel (estuary) was going to be busy so we had to wait till things quieted down and there would be less traffic and relaxed security.

The woman and the girl came through the door with pieces of cheese, baked potatoes, butter, apples and acorn coffee. The little girl hovered over me and smiled the whole time. After the meal, she took me by the hand and led me through the kitchen through another door and down a long flight of stairs to the basement. There was a lighted lantern and she pointed to a bed in the far corner. A dirty pillow and at least three blankets were piled on a homemade bed. I sat down on the bed and the girl patted my knee and scampered up the steps and softly closed the door. I was alone and the quiet was engrossing. Then I remembered Robert and I were separated for the first time.

The next days were spent sleeping, eating and twice a day a walk in a small backyard, always under the supervision of the girl. The girl never spoke, even though I tried to find out what happened to the Frenchman and Hette. The smell of the sea was evident and there was cold fog for the last two days. I was getting my strength back, the food was adequate but not enough of it. The fish was the main staple and I was getting used to it, but didn't know what it was. The walking built up my leg strength and my thoughts were of home, San Francisco. The weather at Den Helder was a lot like that of the city at this time of year. The fog should have been a blessing. I thought it would cover us when we were in the North Sea. Expressing pleasure with the fog, I was rudely told by Robert, that wasn't my business. For my information, fog caused more patrols and more patrols meant more of a chance of being boarded and searched. Even I realized what he was saying. This conversation took place when I was exercising and Robert came into the yard. The young girl kept her eyes on me, but did not come closer.

Robert continued to rebuke me. He really let me have it and finally told me to keep my mouth shut. Before I could vent my rising anger the girl slipped next to me and grabbed my hand, squeezing it. Robert saw that, came up to her, kissed her forehead and patted her head. He whispered, "Christina," and then left the yard. She stood still, still clutching my hand, smiling at me, then led me back to my room. She was about 8 years-old, medium height, braided long brown hair, wearing a faded blue dress and high top shoes. As always, she left me alone and quietly closed the door. As always, I was again alone. Except for Kirsten I was isolated from everything and everyone. This operation was so wild it probably would work, but we had to have luck at every turn. The way the "fleet" was to get across the estuary and into Denmark was yet to be explained to me. Robert had told me the fleet made several trips into the North Seas and the timing of such an excursion was based on several factors: (1) the frequency of the fishing fleet as a group had to be standard not a glaring delay. That would cause an inquiring E-boat captain; (2) the estuary had to be free of traffic from Wilhelmshaven and Hamburg; (3) the weather had to be relatively good, because the formation and navigation had to be precise and not a haphazard number of boats in any widespread group; (4) the E-boats were circling the Dutch boats, but at a respectable distance.

Chapter Eight
The Fishing Fleet

NOVEMBER 17, 1943

The identity and travel papers were taken from me two days ago. They were returned to me this morning while we were having breakfast, consisting of cheese, fried potatoes, hot bread and the inevitable acorn coffee. Not a word was spoken. There still wasn't any sign of Hette or Robert. The little girl sat next to me and ate like the rest of us.

All of us went out the front door with the little girl grabbing my hand and clutching it hard. She led me into the street, staying very close to me. It was foggy and very cold. The wind caused us to turn our backs. The large naval-type jacket helped, but the North Sea was providing a very cold wind.

The group walked for about three miles and came to a wharf leading out into the fog. I heard the lapping of the waves against the wharf pilings. It took us about 30 minutes to get there. I was guessing about the time, for the fog persisted. Other than the water, there was no sounds. I guessed there was no movement from inland because of the loss of visibility. The large man disappeared into the fog. The young girl led me down the wharf. We were surrounded by the fog. I hesitated, but she pulled me forward, still smiling. I could hear her teeth chattering and she felt like she was becoming frantic. I squeezed her hand.

Soon I smelled the odor of fish and gradually the form of a fishing boat appeared out of the gloom. The girl led me aboard the boat by a gangplank and slid a door open and pushed me inside. The boat engine was idling. There were several lights dimly outlining parts of the ship.

She was still holding my cold and sweaty hand. We went below deck and immediately the smell of food was in the air, plus a warmth that thawed me out in no time. The girl was now grinning and rubbed her stomach.

The cook was standing by the wood stove. He smiled at me and placed three cups in front of us and a steaming pot of real coffee. The cook motioned and pointed, then held up four fingers. He pointed to a map table that showed Den Helder and a line through the Waddensee to a village along the North Sea in Holland, Hoorn to be exact. It looked to be about four hours away. The Waddensee was protected by a string of islands.

As we were drinking our coffee (the young girl included), the engine started to accelerate. The boat shook and I heard the movement of feet overhead. The big blonde man was steering the boat. The young girl, still smiling, guided me to the pilot house. The big man was steering the boat way from the wharf. He was concentrating, so he did not notice my entrance. The girl put her finger to my mouth and pointed towards the rear of the boat. I could vaguely see another boat behind us. The girl held up four fingers. Four boats in tandem, all moving slowly. After about 30 minutes, the fog started to lift and I could see the four boats astern. The girl gave me the "thumbs up" and pointed ahead. There was a German E-boat coming our way at slow speed. The girl pushed me to the floor and leaned out of the window waving as the E-boat passed. I peered out and saw the Germans with several machine guns no longer looking at us. As we passed east of the islands we were hugging the coast. There were low clouds and some drizzle, but no rain or snow, although the wind was really chilling as we slowed down (we had been on the water for a long time). The clock in the pilot house indicated we had been moving steadily for four hours. Our heading had been northeast all of the time. As we rounded a hill, a village appeared with several fishing boats and an E-boat tied up to the wharf (with a Nazi flag fluttering in the breeze).

The boat captain said something to the girl in Dutch. She turned to me and pointed to the floor. I was tired of no conversation, so I pointed at me and said, "David." Then I pointed at her and opened my hands. She looked at the boat captain. He nodded. She smiled and said slowly, "Kirsten," then again pointed to the floor. I got down and gave her a thumbs up. We coasted into the jetty and immediately a German guard showed up asking what we wanted. The captain said we had a broken piston and would have to replace it as soon as he could find one in the village. The guard waved him towards the village. As soon as the captain left, Kirsten pointed to the engine room below and indicated we had a spare in the boat by pointing to the storeroom. Then she again gave me a thumbs up, smiled and gazed out of the porthole in the control cabin.

Our boat was tied up amongst the rest of the fishing boats. Two ships from us was a German guard, patrolling the wharf with overhead lights at each ship. Our other three boats were docked down by the sea. Unbeknownst to me, the engineer, who I only saw twice during entire dangerous mission, was already dismantling the engine. I heard several muted sounds from below and saw the engineer with the head of the engine already removed. I opened the floor entrance to the engine room and saw the engineer dismantling the broken piston from the crankshaft. Another piston was on the sideboard. The broken piston was real, but the reason for the ruse could only be for the purpose of letting the captain get into the village and talking with his friends.

The replacing of the piston and replenishment of supplies was going to take several days. Perhaps the most important time element was the approval of the Kriegsmarine that was based on the comings and goings of German ships.

The captain came strolling down the wharf whistling. He had a large paper-wrapped package. Behind him was a small thin gray-haired man. They both came aboard and into the pilot house. Kirsten and I huddled together on the floor. When the little man entered, Kirsten jumped up and embraced him and started crying. The old man was her grandfather, named Hans. They had not seen each other for two years. Kirsten before this year, wanted to participate in resistance activities, but her parents were afraid she was too young. They finally relented when they heard where she was going. This, then, was the opportunity they had hoped for seeing the grandfather. This was Kirsten's first mission. The large blonde ship captain was a member of the Resistance and the uncle of Kirsten. All of this I was told by the grandfather in broken English.

"We have to wait for a week before we can go to the fishing grounds. There is much too much naval activity from Hamburg and Wilhelmshaven. You will have to come to the village with me and hide."

The proximity of the E-boat and the guards was unsettling and I silently agreed with the old man Hans. I was beginning to feel like I was going to gain my freedom, but there were many problems ahead. I nodded and understood the obvious dangers I could think of and only too happy to leave the confines of the boat. Both Kirsten and the captain were watching for my expression and they got it.

The old man looked for my response, but the use of English was quite a shock I couldn't absorb altogether, so I merely nodded my head. The captain nodded and Kirsten smiled a broad smile.

"We will have to leave now. The Germans have strengthed the number of guards to keep onlookers away." I didn't know what that meant and I didn't ask. The old man, Kirsten and I left the boat together. When we passed the naval guard, the old man saluted and said something in German and I slouched. Kirsten held my hand tightly as we passed by. The wharf was very long and I felt like the guard was watching our every move. Fortunately, the fog started to appear in strength, so I tried to relax as we moved towards the village. My clothes were wet again and I was getting cold. Automatically, I slouched down as I had done so many times in the past. My back had been coming along nicely, but the slouching down flared it up again. Kirsten noticed my grimacing and rubbed my arm and walked closer to me. There didn't seem to be any activity in the area. The whole street having no lights, it was difficult to identify the houses, the color, the slope of the roofs or the size. There was no way to tell the number of people in the village, but it was obvious it was a fishing village dependent upon the business of netting fish. Although not in sight, there was a German naval compound that supported the vast E-boat contingent. I was to find out the Dutch Resistance had operated for three years under the noses of the Nazis. The Kriegsmarine was so busy guarding the approaches from the North Sea that they didn't realize the Dutch were running food and guns to their compatriots, but until now, not people. This was, I suspected a vigorous community. The biggest problem the Germans had was they operated during daylight hours and escorted all kinds of ships in and out of the estuary, the main artery for the Germany navy in the northern approaches. The E-boat fleet was quite large and they were busy based on the number of ships coming in and out of the shipyards in Northern Germany. To keep things under control, the town was off-limits and that played right into the hands of the Dutch.

After reaching the darkened street we stopped in front of a building looking the same as the next. The old man, Hans, knocked on the door and almost immediately the door opened and there was a short middle-aged man who in English, ushered us inside. When he had closed the door, said, "You are now in my care. I am Rolf, responsible for you." Then he motioned us up the stairs. At the top of the narrow steps he opened a door and led us in past the sitting room and into the kitchen. The smell of fish and cabbage was evident. An older woman was cooking on an old iron stove (the kind my grandmother had in San Francisco). Rolf said for us to sit down. The older woman brought a bowl of steaming cabbage, fish (looked like bass, when actually it was mackerel or a large perch), boiled potatoes, turnips and real coffee. I couldn't believe what I was seeing. I looked at Kirsten and she was already taking one of the fish and was smiling. The old man, sitting next to her, patted her on the head. The old woman leaned over from the other side and gave her a kiss and patted her head and I relaxed. A real family reunion! At first nothing but the sound of silverware against plates was heard. Then Rolf, as if reading my thoughts, said quietly, "We provide the food for the Nazis and skim some off the top for us." He had a big grin on his face when he said it. Everyone at the table looked at Rolf and he interpreted in Dutch what he had told me and everyone laughed and clapped.

Rolf said something to the girl and she took my hand and led me through the door, up then up another flight of stairs and I found myself in a small bedroom in the attic. There was a small bed, a small water closet, a stool, a small fireplace and a coal scuttle, empty. There was one small window facing the front of the house and the street. Kirsten left, closing the door. I was sitting on the edge of the bed when the bed started shaking and the window rattled with a cracked pane. I ran to the door and started down when the old man was coming up the stairs. He held his hand out to me to stop. He said in a low voice, "Those were the British night fighters coming in very low. They come in every night. Sorry." With that he went back down the stairs and closed the door. I was never on the "dirty end of the stick" before. I didn't like it. I was alone and shaking.

Two days later I was beginning to get nervous. Kirsten appeared at the doorway and motioned me to follow her. Rolf and the captain were there with maps in front of them. Rolf said, "We have decided to tell you what is going on. London has verified who you are (how I will never know)." He then proceeded to brief me on how his fleet (as he called them) was six boats. They were going to the best fishing grounds in Holland. The problem was that the fishing area was also in the exit from the Nazi ships to the North Sea. That's why we had to wait so long and sources only gave us the green light to cross the shipping lane last night. The said the main part of the ships were at Holmwerd, a fishing village on the north coast of Holland waiting for us. It was going to take us five days to get there. He noticed my frown and added "We have had three years to gain the confidence of the Boche. We provide the food for the factory workers so they let us alone for the most part."

Rolf signaled the other boats and all started their engines

and headed, line astern, out into the inland waterway. The next two days were one of furious activity. Rolf had gotten permission from the German command to take his "fleet" to their favorite fishing area after they picked up the rest of the fishing boats. We were heading towards the North Sea protected by the chain of islands leading towards the north. We were starting on a four-day trek and that was boring for me. There was nothing to do but eat, sleep and exercise.

There were no books on the boat, so I busied myself by learning how to operate the sextant, our only means of navigation. During the day I practiced taking "sun shots" and learned how to plot the results on the naval charts. At night I took shots of Polaris, the North Star and learned to plot them also.

It was a way to spend the time and my using a WWI sextant became something to do during the days and nights. Rolf was visibly pleased with my attempt to help and was sure I was well-versed in navigation which I was not. Kirsten beamed and Rolf told me she wanted me to stay with them. I was the "brother" she never had. When the first E-boat approached, Rolf hastily reminded me of my position and to stay out of the open. Kirsten giggled and turned her back.

The next four days went by fairly quickly. We saw several E-boats and Rolf told me we were scrutinized by use of binoculars. They considered us "friendly," and wouldn't take the time to check us by boarding. Kirsten never left my side; we were nearing our destination.

Escape Or Evade

Chapter Nine
The Battle
NOVEMBER 28, 1943

Rolf blew his horn three times and the other five boats went into line abreast. They all started dropping their nets without missing a beat. It was obvious these people knew what to do and when to do it. It was amazing to watch. Three hours later the captain blew his horn twice and the boats hauled in their nets. We had a good catch of sea bass and mackerel. Rolf said the Nazis would check our holds to see the size of the catch before they would allow us to pass into the open sea. We would be escorted by E-boats, "just in case" there were any defectors, as Rolf put it. They had been doing this for a long time, he added and was counting on that complacency when the right time came.

The captain was an "iron man." He never left the bridge for five days and only slept for two hours and then only when the engineer relieved him. Fortunately for us, the engine was purring along. We changed course to the east. Rolf said we were five miles from Holmwerd where we would stay until released by the Germans.

The sea was calm, the weather was fair (some low clouds). The wind was not a problem. The ships clock said it was 6 p.m. and getting dark ahead. I saw the lights of a town. We pulled into a cove and I counted 12 fishing boats and a E-boat. Rolf indicated "this was my fleet," but we would have to get the approval of the Boche before could leave. We docked next to the E-boat, shut down the engines and left the pilot house. We were to the left of the German boat.

The captain was gone for more than an hour. The engineer, Kirsten and I slept on the floor under three blankets. It was cold, but the body heat helped. Rolf came back after what seemed to be an eternity (it was only an hour). He told me they would leave the next day, November 30, if the second E-boat arrived.

It was light when the sound of engines awakened me. I peeked over the rear window and saw an E-boat coming into the jetty. It was 8 a.m. and Rolf appeared outside the pilot cabin. Apparently, he had slept outside. He stuck his head into the room from the sliding door and said we would leave in two hours and that was good. It would take the E-boat that long to refuel and take on water.

At 9:45 the captain signaled the other boats (by a long blast of his horn) to start the engines of the 15 fishing boats. The refueled E-boat and its companion, started toward the open sea. There were already two German patrol boats outside the harbor, but were not moving. The captain said they were there to check on us and to replace the E-boats if anything happened to the two other boats. Very predictable, Rolf said and that he was counting on two E-boats to patrol the 16 fishing boats. That would make it easier for us. He backed the boat out of the jetty as we picked up our navigator. Then we moved out towards the open sea. The navigator shook hands with Rolf who just shook his head. The new crew member merely nodded to Kirsten and me. He must be in on who was on the boat and what was going to happen and more importantly, where we were going. I thought that they must surely be pros at this kind of thing. I found out later, I was the first Allied flyer they had taken, then I remembered the southern escape route had just been compromised just about the time I showed up.

As we left the harbor, our 16 boats shifted to four rows of four boats each. One patrol boat was in front and the other was on the seaward side. Just as we were about to enter the traffic route (our navigator had plotted it on his map) the lead patrol boat fired a red-red flare and we all stopped our engines (maybe they were in idle). Off to our right an E-boat showed up heading west, followed by three submarines, one behind the other. The sight was electrifying. There were the scourge of the Atlantic, leaving their berths to prey on the convoys, mostly American boats and American crews. All of them were doing their part to keep England surviving and fighting. These thoughts flashed across my mind, but I was seized by anger. My hands clenched and I noticed Kirsten was watching me. We had no radios and were powerless to help.

Kirsten whispered to Rolf and without turning his head said in English, "There is nothing we can do. I will report this sighting when I can. It will help. We have seen this before." I said something, but I don't remember what. I continued to stare at those three lethal weapons, German flags waving, painted dark gray, serenely heading towards the war. Frustration overtook me. All I could do was look.

The second patrol boat pulled up and German sailors started to board us. Kirsten pulled three boards from the aft section of the pilot house and literally pushed me into a space that I barely fit and then she re-inserted the boards. I couldn't turn around and I couldn't sit down. I heard the soldiers talking to the navigator. By the time they left, my back was giving me a bad time, but there was nothing I could do but stand there and bear the pain! I started to sweat in what seemed like an eternity, I was so cramped, I don't think I could have stood being in that position very much longer. As the Germans departed, Kirsten pulled out the false wallboards and pulled me out. Tears were running down my cheeks from the back pain. I almost collapsed. The captain sat me down. I pointed to my back and Kirsten started rubbing it, nodding her head. I put my head between my legs and the pain gradually subsided. I looked up and saw the E-boat move off. The submarines were slowly moving to the west. I remember thinking the Beaufighters should have been there (these were RAF coastal command planes on the east coast of Great Britain).

Several minutes later, the lead patrol boat fired a green flare and the fishing fleet started to move northward again. Once we passed the travel lane, all of our boats threw out their nets. It was getting late because of our stopping, but we kept going, dragging our nets. The E-boat, almost invisible because of the time of day, flashed his search light and started a fast turn to the right (east); our boat started to follow, but Rolf rammed the throttles forward and we picked up speed immediately. The navigator gave our captain a new heading. Kirsten's smile broadened and she slapped me on the back. We were making a run for Denmark! It was obvious to me this had been pre-planned by Rolf and his boat captains. The timing (approaching darkness and the location of the E-boat) was perfect and it appeared our luck was holding. The boat surged forward. The engines vibrated the whole area. Rolf had turned to the heading given to him by the navigator. It happened so fast the navigator must have calculated what and when the escape was going to happen. He gave Rolf the new heading as if it were a planned maneuver, that it was.

The compass spun, then settled down. We were making a run and I lost sight of the E-boat. It looked as if we were on our way. The engineer had extinguished all of the lights except those in the pilot house and the boat had accelerated now making large bow waves.

As we were in the center of the estuary picking up speed, the sound of aircraft engines suddenly were readily apparent from the southwest. The patrol boat on the left suddenly appeared not to hear the engines with their powerful engines drowning out what was near them, but behind them and the fleet. The noise of all the boat's engines were drowning out what I was hearing.

Suddenly, three British Beaufighters (with distinctive roundels) in a loose formation below the low overcast, appeared just above the sea. The leading E-boat was turning east, but they saw the aircraft and started firing their 40mm guns, but the two Beaus were heading towards Wilhelmshaven. The third one banked steeply to the right, came right over us and started shooting its six 20mm guns at the patrol boat on our left. It was close enough to us to see the discarded empty shell casings raining down and hitting the water. He was going so fast he only got a split second to shoot, but he was hitting the German craft several times above the waterline. As he whipped overhead I read his identification, "RRV" in red over the camouflaged fuselage.

In a tight, swift turn he came back over us and poured a heavy bust into the patrol boat. It started to burn in the rear, but the gunners were till firing from the boat. All of a sudden, the boat exploded showering us with debris. The Beaufighter banked back west still hugging the sea. The pilot was outstanding and he was in control all of the time.

It was all over in about a minute, but seemed an eternity. I gasped for breath. I realized I had held my breath during the encounter. The other E-boat was still firing at the fighter with its 40mm guns, but I could see the shot hitting the water short of the British fighter. My heart was pounding and I yelled as loudly as I could. Kirsten was on the floor of the pilot house and Rolf was all smiles. He kept control of his boat and didn't change course one degree.

The Beaufighter pilot and crew were "on the deck," but waggled his wings as he went out of sight. I'm sure he realized what he had "stumbled on" and took advantage of the situation. Still, I wondered what and where his target was originally. Also, what happened to the other two. I never found out, but hopefully they hit their targets and returned safety.

The attempt to get away, the submarines stumbled on, the Beaufighters, the strafing, the loss of the patrol boat, all were overwhelming. I looked over at the corner of the pilot compartment and saw Kirsten huddled with her knees against her chest, head down and trembling. I reached over and stroked her head. Then, I patted the shoulder of the navigator. He smiled. I grabbed the right arm of Rolf.

The other boats kept turning back south, pulling in their nets filled with fish. We pulled ours in but kept going north without lights. I looked at our map and the navigator's finger was on a small seaport of Ribe on the southwest coastline of

Denmark. I expressed concern for the safety of our boat, but Rolf said not to worry, he would tell the Boche his steering jammed! He smiled and patted me on the head.

As I looked back, the fishing fleet had scattered in all directions. Once the British attack was over several of the patrol boats were apparently searching for German survivors. I found out an E-boat had a crew of seven (pilot, navigator, engineer and four gunners). Two men were picked up and returned to Holmwerd, our departure point.

Rolf told me his people rescued the Germans for two reasons: (1) they didn't want to see any normal soldiers die immediately; (2) the Dutch wanted the Germans to know they were good people. In this way, they hoped they would be able to continue the fishing, for the people.

The nets were pulled in and we had another good catch that would end up in Denmark, but that couldn't be helped. With the two engines pounding we were moving very fast. Ten hours later we pulled into the harbor of Ribe. We turned on our running lights about an hour before we reached port. Everything had gone just like they had planned.

We slowed down and pulled up to the wharf. Several men were there and they knew we were coming. We found out later a heavy fog had moved in and the patrol boats and the fishing fleet barely made it back to Holmwerd and that was why we were not chased. We got in port about 3 a.m. Kirsten came with me when three men motioned me to follow them. I was exhausted and wanted to sleep.

Chapter Ten

Denmark

NOVEMBER 30, 1943

From the time we left the fishing fleet behind and before we came into view of our Denmark destination, I had time to review just how lucky the Germans were even though they lost two patrol boats. Had the Beaufighters been 10 minutes earlier, three submarines could have been lost. As it was I didn't understand how the Beaufighters missed the subs, but I guess that is another story. I can only assume the submarines saw the three fighters and crash-dived.

As we came off the wharf, I saw the now familiar German uniforms and unconsciously stooped over. Rolf was on one side, putting his arm over my shoulders and Kirsten on the other side holding my hand and squeezed it hard. Rolf leaned over and said quietly, "My young friend, the worst is over. You are almost at freedom's gate. It is good for both of us." With that, he turned and headed back to the ship. I inadvertently slowed down and looked back over my shoulder. Kirsten yanked me and we moved past the soldiers. They were talking to each other and didn't want me to slow down and give them a good look at me.

As we left the long wharf, Kirsten pulled me right and we were on a dirt road. I was clearly disappointed and very tired, but keep on following Kirsten. There were many things I wanted to say to Rolf, plus my profound thanks for his expertise in getting me out of a very difficult position. I was determined she would not get away, expressing my feelings toward all of them.

We came up to the tail of a medium-sized truck and Kirsten motioned me into the front cab of the truck. She got in the cab next to me. When Kirsten closed the door, the driver was looking straight ahead and he moved the truck out. We were going quite fast through a small town, Kolding, without slowing down.

Past the town we turned off onto a side road and pulled into a medium-sized barn with two men holding open the door. The driver shut down the engine, turned to me smiling. He said in good English, "I am Paul Aanstad. Welcome to Denmark and welcome to my folk's farm." Short and sweet.

The two people holding the doors were standing there and the man extended his hand and the woman kissed me on my cheek. They both touched me. Paul said they had never been near an American. My height surprised them. They were about five feet, six inches and I was six feet and three inches. Paul hugged his parents. They whispered for about a minute. Paul turned to me and said, "We will be here three days and you will sleep in the barn," then pushed me towards the small one-story house. It started to snow, but not too badly. Paul opened the door to the house and I motioned his folks to go ahead. They both smiled and slapped me on the shoulder. Then Kirsten went in and I followed her. The entrance led into a kitchen. There was a tall blonde woman at the stove with her back to me. The table was set for a meal. It was obvious we were expected. The aroma of chicken, bread and cabbage made my mouth water. Temporarily, my exhaustion was forgotten.

The tall blonde woman turned and looked at me with the bluest eyes I have ever seen. She smiled and the look on my face gave me away. She was gorgeous. She spoke, grinning and blushing at the same time, "I am Paul's sister. I am called Eva. My name is Evangeline." She turned back to the stove and started dishing up the food. I stood there with my mouth open, but speechless. Paul said to sit down. I ate like I hadn't eaten a full meal for days. The chicken was boiled and delicious. The boiled potatoes had a taste I had not tasted before. There was huge bowl in the center of the table containing boiled cabbage. It was not overcooked, thank goodness. The fresh bread was steaming hot and there was beer in tall glasses in front of each of us.

Kirsten drank down the glass of beer without taking a deep breath. It was obvious she had had beer before. I slid my glass over to her (I don't drink beer) and she drank half of it and reached for the chicken. Paul and Eva smiled and shook their heads. For the most part Eva kept her eyes on me and it was embarrassing, but I didn't complain. She looked to be around 25. She was a real beauty. Being younger didn't bother me, although the thought crossed my mind.

The warmth of the room was overpowering. We finished our meal and Paul offered me a small cigar. I declined, saying I wanted to lie down and sleep. Paul got up and went outside. I followed him and Eva followed me! She had a bundle she was holding. Paul led me to the back of the barn and pointed to a large stack of hay. There were two cows leisurely eating hay and there was a bucket of water nearby. Paul said to burrow my way in behind the cows. Eva stepped forward and holding the bundle towards me told me to take off my clothes. She said to hand her my old clothes. I found it only too accommodating and threw her my stinking clothes gladly.

My new clothes consisted of a heavy gray shirt, a dark blue turtleneck sweater, black pants, thick socks and a pair of thick woolen underwear that had been patched several times. Paul and Eva would take the smelly clothes and burn them. She picked them up and pinched her nose, smiling and went away. The mother and father had disappeared. Paul patted me on the head and said, "Sweet dreams."

Escape Or Evade

Chapter Eleven
Evangeline
DECEMBER 1-2, 1943

hen I awoke the next morning it was light and snowing. I realized Kirsten was not there and I got mad. Making my way out of the barn I sneezed several times and the cows snorted to let me know I had disturbed them. The snow was still falling and had accumulated about 12 inches on the ground. I noted there were footprints coming and going from the house. There was also a path from the house to what I thought was a chicken coop. It didn't look much like a coop. Much too much elaborate.

I went to the door and knocked. The mother opened the door, grabbed me and pulled me in. She obviously was afraid of the possibility the Germans were in the area. The heat was a welcome surprise. Paul, the mother, father and Kirsten were sitting at the table. Eva looked great pouring me a cup of coffee, holding onto my shoulders and said to help myself to eggs, hot bread and sausages, heavily spiced. I felt like I was in heaven. Surprisingly, there was no salt or pepper. The eggs were all sunnyside up, but tasted delicious with the buttered bread. We used to call that "sopping good."

Eva sat down and while eating told me I had to take a bath when I finished. I thought she was a fussy one. I found out later the Danes are very clean. The use of steam baths was almost a national institution. Almost every home had one. I asked for my old clothes and she said she had burned them and pinched her nose in disgust, smiling. Then she said she could cut my hair (it was getting scruffy and long. Most of the people had crew cuts). Kirsten looked as though she would "bust a gut," snickering, but said nothing.

My days were spent feeding the chickens and pigs, after Eva taught me the correct way. It was a most enjoyable time. The snow had stopped and there were no Germans around. One could almost forget there was war on. On the other hand, I wanted to get back to my outfit. A 20 year-old isn't too smart.

On the third day, Paul brought me a wool suit, a very worn shirt, knickers, long colored stockings (quite faded) and a well-worn fedora hat. We would leave the next day. Arrangements had been made. Smiling, he said Eva wanted to see me now.

With my bundle of clothes, I went to the house. The snow was almost gone. The sun was out and it was a beautiful day. I went into the house and there was Eva and Kirsten. They took my new clothes, grabbed me by the hands and led me to a door at the far end of the kitchen. Kirsten opened the door and there was an old fashioned bathtub, brimming with steaming hot water. Eva handed me a bar of handmade soap and pointed to the tub. We all stood there looking at each other. Finally, for fear the water was getting cold, I asked what was going on. Eva threw up her hands and said in a strong voice, "Take off your clothes and get in the bath." I didn't know the Danes thought nothing of seeing one of the other sex taking a bath. Kirsten, a Belgian, didn't move or say anything. She just stared.

Three hours later and 10 pounds of dirt removed (exaggeration - but I sure felt lighter), I put on my new suit opened the door and said in a loud voice, "Here I am you lucky people." I felt good and showed it. The mother had her back turned cooking eggs, bacon and warming the bread. Kirsten was feeding the stove with logs. There was milk, coffee and butter on the table. Eva was staring at me intently and just shrugged her shoulders.

Eva came in from outside and gave me a long hand-knitted muffler, saying the Copenhagen train had no heat. She said Paul was to take me to the Copenhagen train at 11:30 a.m. the next day, November 30. No one said anything. Paul then said we would go to Nyborg and then take a ferry to Slagelse. He said nothing about where we were going from there (I presumed from the last discussion, it would be Sweden). I didn't have time to think about it, although internment was on my mind. Kirsten took my hand and led me to the barn. It was about 4 p.m., December 2 and she pushed me into the hay. She crawled in behind me. By this time I had arranged a cave in the thick hay. Kirsten laid down beside me and we kept each other warm.

Chapter Twelve

Copenhagen

DECEMBER 3, 1943

I didn't think I slept too well, but had to rustle myself awake at 9 a.m. I stumbled to the house. Kirsten was not in sight. Mother was fixing breakfast. Paul and Eva were at the table. Paul announced Kirsten had left early this morning on her way back to Belgium. That was a shock. I never heard or saw her again. That was a real shock. It seems they come and they go without any fanfare.

I forced myself to eat a hearty breakfast (because of what we were scheduled to do) and left by two-wheeled cart to the train station at Holding. We got there early and Eva got the tickets for Paul, her and me. The locals were queuing up for the train to Copenhagen. On the platform I stayed close to my friends and again scrunched down. The people were talking loudly and the train rolled in promptly at 11:30 a.m. As the train stopped everyone rushed to the third class compartments. Paul, Eva (with her arm through mine) and I sauntered to the first class carriage and climbed aboard. As we sat down the conductor came through the door and collected our tickets. He tipped his hat and moved on.

The train was the same as those before, but there was a noticeable absence of Germans. I knew Denmark was occupying the role of being controlled but it was different than in Holland, Belgium and France. For some reasons, the Danes had a different attitude towards their captors. I believe that was because they hadn't had to withstand the continuous abuse of what the other countries were subjected to.

The lack of control by the Nazis was playing right into the hands of the Danish Resistance (the Germans believed they could provide a lot more for less military) by their overt acquiescence. The Danish people's real beliefs were not publicized and their retaliation was not as extensive, but they did what they had to do to survive.

The way the conductor acted was the first tip-off to the lack of Nazi control outside of the big cities. The indifference was evident whether real or connived. Eva sat close to me and Paul opposite. She held my hand and it was very reassuring. Paul kept looking out of the window.

I couldn't help but look at Eva. She was tall, had long blonde hair and was beautiful. She was looking out of the window on the other side of the aisle. She slowly turned her head and looked directly at me with those huge blue eyes. She smiled, grabbed my hand and winked, so as to say, "we're on our way and no problems." She then closed her eyes and went to sleep. It was a good idea and I leaned against the window and the swaying of the train car soon had me napping.

We arrived at Odense at 2:45 p.m., left the train, but were late getting to the ferry boat so we had two hours to wait. We wandered from the station into the town of Nyborg. Almost immediately we saw a restaurant and entered. The first thing we saw were two German officers talking over coffee. They didn't even look up. As we sat next to them, it was obvious their proximity was a shelter. Paul explained why we did this, in as much as there were a lot of empty tables. Thirty excruciating minutes later the Germans left, glancing at Eva as they passed by. I didn't realize I was holding my breath. Eva punched me in the ribs. I relaxed and drank my coffee in one gulp. Eva punched me again, but grinned at me.

Being at an impressionable age, I knew this woman was something special. We left the restaurant at 4:15 p.m. and the ferry was already there. We got tickets and Paul said the ferry would leave at 5 p.m. heading for Slagsee where we would catch a local train to Copenhagen. The ferry lurched forward. We were headed for a little town of Kohge (?). The train was there at 8 p.m. and the captain wanted to be sure the people would get on the train in time.

We were sitting in the back of the ferry. The seating was by benches and we sat near a window. I stared out and Eva patted my knee and said in a whisper, "Not to worry. We are going to make it and are almost home free. I am going to take good care of you."

The ferry docked at exactly 8 p.m. and we ran towards the train station. Fortunately, the train from the south was late. Paul got the tickets for Copenhagen, came back and flopped down. Eva and I were exhausted from our run. He said it was 90 kilometers to Copenhagen, but we would exit the train short of the big city. He hadn't been this route before and had no idea how many checks there would be, so we would get off early about 10:45. Eva put her hand in mine and I patted her knee, all for the benefit of the two men sitting across from us. Eva was flushed. I closed my eyes and waited.

I started to calculate what had happened. I was shot down and captured November 19 and today was December 3. I had taken 16 days to get where I was. It didn't seem possible to have taken that long. I am sure that time would be shortened in the future.

Each one of the resistance people had been dedicated and to save an Allied flier, on a new untested route was unbelievable. The route was going to be refined, but to have to grope their way every day with a novice was almost unacceptable, except for those people who were told a new route for an escapee was not feasible. From Professor Bergeron to Rolf, these rare individuals hopefully would survive the war and return to their home and families.

There appeared to be an air of relaxed apprehension while we were in Denmark. I never really understood why, but it helped me to relax. The tension of being out of control and being controlled by other forces (both friendly and unfriendly) is difficult to describe. It was frustrating on their side, the Resistance was doing a job, their way of confronting the invaders. We were a commodity who required the country's people to protect them. It was ludicrous. We were fighting the oppressors from the air and the oppressed were doing their best to keep us going. It was weird, but comforting.

The train arrived and we stumbled into a compartment. Eva and I sat on one side and Paul on the other. I was exhausted and fell asleep on Eva's shoulder as the train started moving. She woke me up and said to be prepared to get off. It was 10:50 p.m. outside of Copenhagen. She said Paul would continue on and make arrangements to get me to Sweden! As the train stopped again, we got off and made for the exit. We walked for about 20 minutes. In the outskirts, Copenhagen was ginger-bread apartments and narrow streets. I was quiet and the street lights were illuminated, so the cobblestone streets were easy to follow.

Eva walked up to a door in an ordinary looking apartment house. She knocked several times and stepped back. People walked by behind us. She knocked again, harder. On the third knock the door opened and there was a short, black-haired woman, disheveled in a housecoat. They hugged each other and both of them chattered for several minutes. I got nervous and coughed. Eva looked at me and led me into the house. Once the door closed the woman and Eva burst into laughter! Eva introduced the woman as Ilse, one of her college friends. Eva continued, saying Ilse was not part of the Danish Resistance, but was very sympathetic with the Allies, especially America. She went on to say Ilse's brother was going to college now in Florida. Her only regret was that he couldn't come back home until the war was over.

Ilse's husband was an engineer who worked in the north and knew nothing about Ilse's part in this operation. I showed my concern and was assured her husband, Peter, would be sym-pathetic and could be counted upon to support his wife and might even help, if possible. I looked at Eva and she put her head down. I knew she had gotten Ilse into an uncompromis-ing position, but counted on her to protect me. Her Peter was another story, I was uneasy. Time would tell and I trusted Eva to do the right thing.

We went up a narrow staircase and entered a sitting room. Eva said Ilse was a city bus driver and her husband was "to the North." She said Paul had called and said the British Consulate was too closely watched by the Nazis, but the Americans were "very sympathetic" with my problem and would work out something within a couple of days. In the meantime, I was to "stay put" and not to go outside. That was clear enough, but disappointing. Now, I had to wait again. Ilse, sensing my disappointment and frustration, turned on the radio. There was nice Danish (?) music and she said she would get coffee and cakes.

We sat silently listening to the music with our own thoughts. Ilse came back flushed and spoke to Eva in Danish. Then they both giggled. Eva said my identity was confirmed (Paul called downstairs) and the Ambassador in the American Consulate said I had to get to Malmo, Sweden on my own.

The Americans said they couldn't acknowledge my existence for my protection. Further, Sweden was neutral and they would cooperate but neither would say anything about me if asked. Things were getting complicated. I sat there and waited for somebody to say something.

Eva, realizing my thoughts said, "You can stay here for as long as you want. You don't have to leave. I will stay with you." I was speechless. Eva came and sat beside me resting her head on my shoulder. I got up and walked to the window and looked at the street. There were no Germans in sight. I could hear a plane and the phone rang downstairs and I wondered what was going on.

Ilse came upstairs and announced Paul had called again. He said we were back in business and would come here to explain. Waiting was getting harder to accept, every time there was a delay. Security seemed too flexible.

Some 45 minutes later there was a knock on the door and moments later Paul came in. I was standing by the sofa. Paul pushed me down and said to listen and ask no questions. He acted very excited. I was to find out why shortly. "You have to be on the south taxiway at exactly 2 p.m. December 8th." Today was December 3rd, five days to get away. I thought my blood pressure was noticeably higher. "We are working on a plan to have a small boat pick you up tomorrow, spirit you down the Kategat and get you to Sweden." He went on to say that departure would be set within 24 hours. There was only one problem and that was to find a boat and captain who would help us. Paul left saying he would be back within the next two days. Eva went downstairs to talk to him.

Ilse came and told me we were in no danger and left to get our dinner. Eva did not come back upstairs. Soon I could smell fish and I was immediately hungry. I walked down the stairs to the kitchen and the two women were cooking over a cast iron wood stove. Eva looked at me, winked and then went back to her cooking. Ilse did not look at me. I asked if I could have a cup of coffee and Eva without looking around, pointed to the coffee pot on the stove.

Paul came back the next day. He said I would be leaving tonight at 8 p.m. by a small fishing boat that had used the inlet for fishing for several years and was well-known to the Germans. As we sat down for our meal, Paul told me I would have to trust Hans, the boat owner, but he insisted he couldn't take anyone with him. That was a shock, but Paul said Hans operated by himself and a passenger would be suspicious.

Chapter Thirteen

Sweden and Home

DECEMBER 7-9, 1943

*A*fter dinner I was told to take a nap. It would probably be the last time I would get to sleep for several days. I was so tense I didn't think I could close my eyes, let alone sleep, but at least I could relax.

I started up the stairs and Eva was right behind me. Entering the upper room, I flopped down on the bed. To my surprise, Eva came to the other side of the bed and laid down beside me putting her arm across my chest and her head on my shoulder. She smelled so good. I closed my eyes and drifted off to sleep, my tenseness had evaporated. Her female odor was almost overpowering. She knew I had to go back to my unit, but neither of us said anything.

Eva woke me at 8 p.m. and said quietly it was time to go. Paul was waiting downstairs. She said Hans would guide me to the boat, a distance of about two miles and we'd leave at 10 p.m.

I don't know why but I asked Eva if she was satisfied with the way things were going. Her eyes widened and she leaned over and kissed me, stroking my cheek. Then she got up and walked to the door. I followed her. When we reached the kitchen, Ilse gave me a cup of coffee and introduced me to Hans, a small man who looked to be in his 50s.

He seemed pleasant. Hans said we would have no problems with the Boche, so we didn't have anything to worry about, but we should get going. I drank my coffee, shook hands with Paul and Ilse. Eva said she would see us to the door. Hans went first, me second, then Eva. She hugged me hard and slipped me a piece of paper in my pocket, shoved me through the door and I suddenly was alone except for Hans.

After our good-bye, I held hands with Eva for a moment and gave her a note. She nodded and put her hands in her pocket.

My note said to write my mother. Give her the name and address and tell her they had a common friend and to write. I knew Eva's brother was in Arizona so the Germans wouldn't think anything was amiss with another short note, this time to California.

After returning to the bomb group, I wrote my mother and asked her if she had heard from Denmark. She said "no." I never heard from Evangeline.

Hans motioned me to come with him. We walked through the narrow streets and then started downhill. I could hear the water lapping against the shore and I knew we were close to the boat. It was dark after we left the street. Suddenly, I saw a small wharf and a powerboat snuggled against the dock.

Once aboard, Hans gave me a rolltop sweater and started the engine. The pilot house clock said 10 p.m. Amazing. We went around several small islands and at 1 a.m. we went aground and he said, "Head northeast for about three miles and you will see the air base. Move towards the taxiway lights until you see the runway lights. Find somewhere to hide. A RAF Mosquito will come down the taxiway and flash his landing lights three times and stop. The door in the front of the fuselage will open and you will have 30 seconds to get on board. If you don't make it you will have to come back here and we will have to try again." With that he pushed me onto the shore and waved good-bye and gave a me "V" sign. I left immediately. I didn't hear his engine, so I imagined he would wait for awhile.

I ran up the hill, stopped and found the North Star and gauged northeast. I walked rapidly two miles and I could see the blue taxiway lights ahead. I could see the runway lights. I found some thick buses fairly near the taxiway about 30 yards away. The time was about 2 a.m., by my estimate.

I had no way of knowing the exact time, so I lay prone in the bushes and waited. The appointed time was 2 p.m., 10 hours.

At various times planes taxied to the runway, but none stopped. I tried to relax and wait. Hans had given me a ham and cheese sandwich. I ate it with relish, then remembered Eva had put something in my pocket. She had written a note, "We'll see each other again after the war. Love, Evangeline." That made me nervous.

Just as it was getting warmer, another plane taxied down the taxiway. It stopped short of the runway, flashed the landing lights three times, the hatch opened and a metal ladder came down. I stumbled, then ran to the nose of the Mosquito and scampered up the hatch. A RAF crewman (navigator) pulled me up the ladder into the aircraft, slapped me on the back and pulled/stowed the ladder, closing the hatch. He yelled to the pilot and we moved onto the runway. I heard the increased sound of the engines and we moved down the runway. Once airborne I heard wheels slamming into the wheelwells. I found a seat belt, fastened it. By this time we were in a steep climb. There was a dim light overhead and I saw a cloth helmet and put it on. I heard the pilot talking to the tower station, he was airborne and going off frequency.

The sun was at it highest point and the pilot looked back, gave me a thumbs up and said over the interphone, "Welcome aboard, Yank. Next stop London."

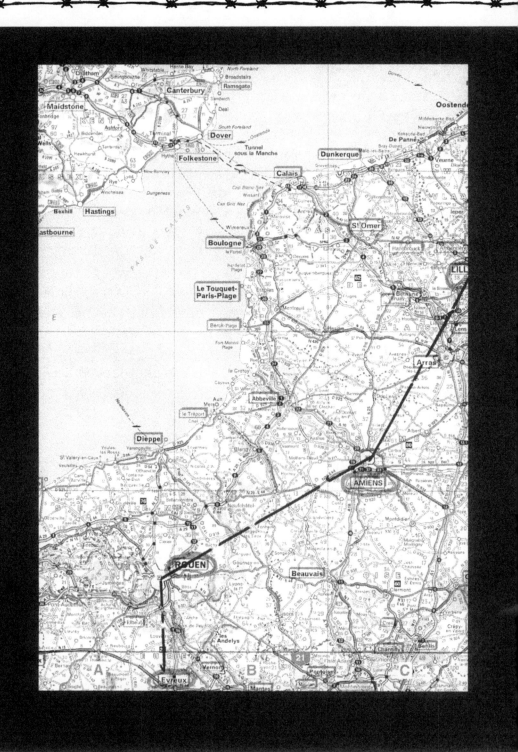

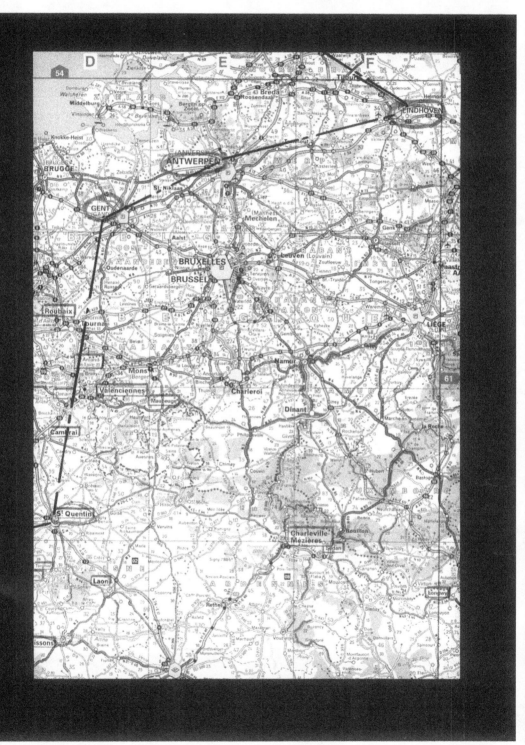

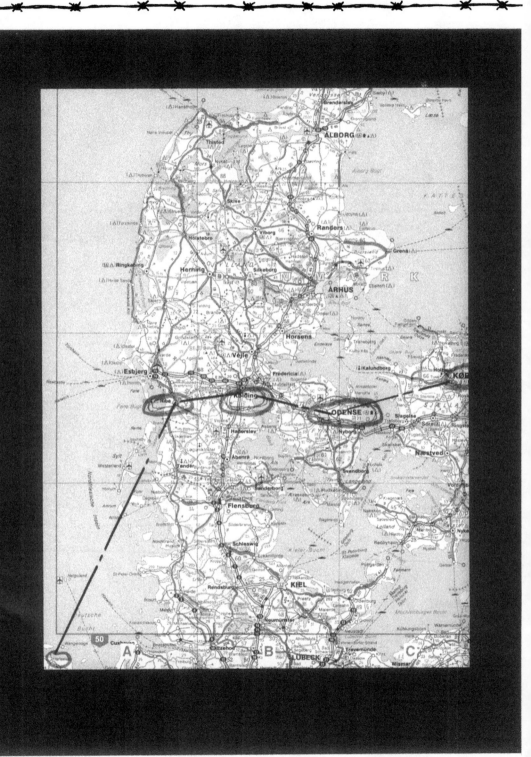

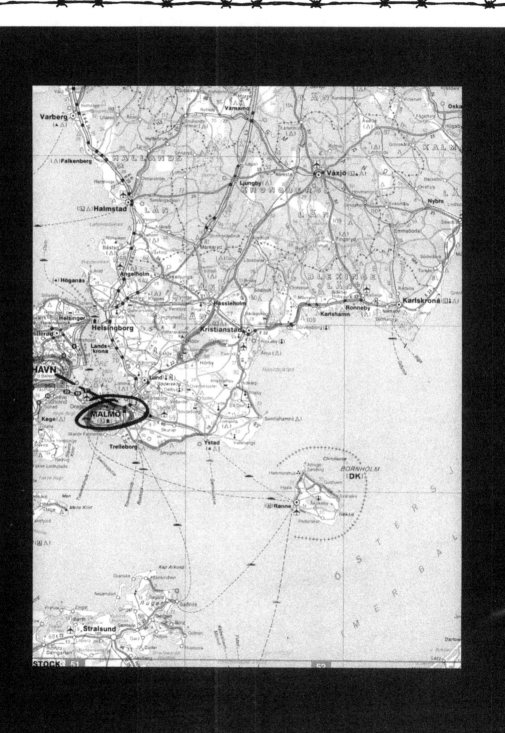

Epilogue

*I*f the reader wonders why I can remember what happened 52 years ago with such clarity, it was because I was inter rogated during the Berlin Airlift, 1948-49. I had to write down the specifics by an Intelligence Officer from Supreme Headquarters Allied Expeditionary Force (SHAEF) and kept my notes all these years. What he did with the information I never was told. I assume it was to award recognition to those who helped and saved us.

After reconstructing this story, I realize I was too critical of the Resistance. It is easy to forget that at the early part (1943) of the European War, the Allies had used the southern route to Spain or in some cases Switzerland, over the Pyrannes Mountains primarily because that route was shorter and had been established when France was fighting both internally (Vichy) and the Germans. The route, initially, was not occupied with actual war activities.

Unfortunately, literally no interest was shown in escapees taking an arduous trip, subsequently called the northern route. If the individual undertook to go to Belgium, Holland, Denmark or Norway, the danger was much worse. Also, there was no coordination between countries (and languages) until the southern route was compromised because the people who operated it got careless, whereas the new routes were a cautious collaboration, a hit-or-miss attempt before the established a secure route.

What is surprising in the movement north, is that Sweden was the exit point. Other than Finland (under Russian influence) Sweden was (is) a neutral country. Norway was under German domination with little support to escapees.

Sweden, on the other hand had to detain the Allied fliers who openly landed in their country in order to maintain their freedom from the Nazis. As a sort of "underground" system, the Swedish officials didn't acknowledge the escaping people if they weren't "aware" they were in their country. Sounds strange, but you had to be there.

Being one of the first to use the "new" route, I now understand what those valiant warriors went though to protect those of us who were fortunate enough to being put in contact with that organization. I realize they were "feeling" their way and hopefully survived.

When I was flying the Berlin Airlift from Frankfurt, West Germany in 1948-49, I went to Copenhagen and tried to find Evangeline. I found the apartment in southern Copenhagen, but the present residents had never heard of Ilse, her husband, Eva, Paul or Hans. The Danish Internal Affairs Office couldn't help me without the surnames, that was never mentioned from the outset. I can only hope Eva is safe and happily growing old.

Note: Prior to 1986, the Air Force considered a flier who was captured by the enemy a prisoner of war (POW), IF he was in enemy hands for more than 30 days.

In 1986 the Veterans Administration (VA) changed the rules. It now states that "a veteran who while on active duty was forcibly detained by a foreign government," without any reference to time of detention.

During 1942-45, the 8th Air Force (England) considered any flier who was captured and escaped in less than 30 days was considered an Evadee. As such could be returned to combat flying status even though the Nazis put a $10,00 bounty on each of us.

After several years of arguing with the Air Force and VA, I was awarded the POW Medal. This book is dedicated to all of the Freedom Fighters of WWII and especially those who helped me, especially Evangeline. I still have the note.